Gerd Ludwig

My Dream Cat

Photos: Ulrike Schanz
Illustrations:
György Jankovics

BARRON'S

CONTENTS

WHAT CATS ARE LIKE

- They form a close relationship with "their" person.

- They are adaptable, but they don't give up their autonomy.

- They need familiar sur-roundings and a predict-able routine.

- They sleep a lot and for long periods, so they are very active when they are awake.

- They need closeness, attention, and affection.

- They like soft voices and slow movements.

- They can listen attentively, and they have trust and warmth to contribute.

People are of two minds when it comes to cats; some are ill at ease, for they perceive cats to be strong willed, contrary, and unpredictable. Others embrace cats as the perfect house pet. The numbers speak for themselves: the league of cat lovers is on the rise. There are millions of cats living in North American households. Cats have long since surpassed dogs and all other house pets in people's estimation.

You might assume that we know everything about an animal that is kept by so many people and that lives so intimately with us. However, even after thousands of years of partnership with humans, cats remain unfamiliar friends. Their unaccustomed behavior and astonishing sense perceptions still are puzzles to us, and our prejudices still bar the way to total rapprochement. In order to build a harmoni-ous partnership with a cat, you need to understand its behavior, its "language," and its needs. This "animal advisor" will help you to find your own dream cat.

HELP IN DECIDING IF CATS

1 House cats can live to be fifteen, twenty, or even twenty-five years old. When you get a cat, you are taking on a long-term responsibility.

2 Kittens bring lots of life into the house, but in the first few weeks, they require constant attention.

3 Whether you get your cat from an animal shelter or from a private source, grown cats already have established ideas about life. It will take patience and time to get them adjusted to their new home.

4 Cats are creatures of habit. Every change in the familiar surroundings and daily routine is an abomination to them.

5 Should you choose a purebred or an ordinary house cat? The decision is subject to personal preference, for there are no major differences in the behavior of the two types. But some breeds require lots of care (see Breed Profiles, pages 16 through 19).

6 In order for indoor cats, in particular, to feel comfortable, they need a home that's set up with their needs in mind (see pages 10–11).

7 Cats often tear through the house playing wild games, and leave hair behind on carpets and cushions; they may even sharpen their claws on the sofa, despite your best efforts to prevent it. You have to be able to take all this in stride.

8 Are you allergic to cat hair? Before you get a cat, it's a good idea to have all family members tested.

ARE FOR YOU

A cat will change your life! A cat places demands on you, requires closeness, affection, care, and attention. Cats are extremely adaptable, but in contrast to dogs, they decide for themselves how and when to make compromises. With dogs, the foundation of a harmonious life together is broad-based and firm obedience training, but with cats, training according to any fixed program is rarely successful. Cats require many more attempts to establish togetherness.

Our advice on cat ownership will help you by answering the most important questions about living with a cat. You need to resolve three essential points before getting a cat:

✔ The decision to get a cat has to be unanimous among all the people who are going to live with it.

✔ A cat costs money. Over the course of the years the costs of acquisition, housing, feeding, care, accessories, visits to the vet, and many other things really add up. Are you ready and able to take on these costs without reservation?

✔ Not everything is peaches and cream in a cat's life. Old, sick cats need lots of attention and care. That takes time, energy, patience, and the willingness to provide some types of support that may not be very pleasant.

THE CAT WORLD AND
THE HUMAN WORLD

Cats like people. They willingly live with people under the same roof, and they offer friendship and warmth. A cat relates with its owner more intimately than with other cats. Just the same, cats remain independent, and they will never try to curry favor or beg for your goodwill.

What's Typical in a Cat?

Cats are the ultimate predator. Cats are perpetual infants. Cats are capable of all kinds of inconsistencies: In living with humans they remain babies for their whole lives, and they expect to be cared for and pampered. Outdoors, when they are on the prowl for prey, they demonstrate that they are confident hunters. In the care of humans, cats have preserved the legacy of wildness inherited from their ancestors, but at the same time, they have recognized that they can trust people and enjoy their protection and care.

Before you embark on living with a cat, you need to learn what its body, character, and behavior are like.

Cats are gifted physically. They can stalk, sprint, gallop, jump far and high, climb, and balance. They are extremely elegant in their movements and amazingly self-assured.

Cats from the same litter get along well together. But a human is even more important to a cat.

Cats are born hunters. Even when they are asleep, cats can hear the movements of a mouse, and they instantly awaken, ready for action. Anything that is small and runs away triggers hunting behavior. That applies even when they join us in playing with a stuffed mouse, a Ping-Pong ball, or a ball of paper.

Cats like cleanliness. The cat bath that people refer to is really an intensive washup. Healthy cats clean themselves regularly and after every meal. Afterward, there may be a discreet scent left from the slightly acidic saliva that the cat spreads over its fur, using its tongue and paws.

Cats are loners with a sociable streak. Cats aren't pack animals like dogs, but social contact is still vitally important to them. That applies to youthful friendships among male cats and to the lifelong need to cuddle among the females in a litter.

Cats are self-assured. Cats that live in the wild have to make decisions on their own, and often instantaneously in order to experience success in hunting or to get away from enemies. House cats haven't had to learn how to do that. But they still know ways to get what they want from their humans – for example by cuddling or meowing pathetically.

What Do Cats Need?

Cats are very adaptable. They can feel comfortable with a wide variety of living conditions and people. A cat can feel at home in a tiny garret or in a barn behind the farmhouse; it gets along with single people who are away at work during the day; it puts up with noisy, large families, clumsy little children, and the annoying dogs in the neighborhood. A cat lover of course doesn't stretch the cat's adaptability to the breaking point, but rather knows how to make it happy:

✔ Cats need fixed times for rest, play, and feeding. In the final analysis, they are pedantic creatures that are not inclined to make compromises. If you don't respect their needs, they can find ways to protest (see pages 36–37).

✔ Cats need private space. In order to be happy, cats need a place to sleep where they won't be disturbed; food and water dishes where there's no competition from other cats or from a dog; a litter box that's not in public view; and some cardboard boxes where they can hide.

Everything a cat needs, from scratching post to cat grass.

✔ Cats need cuddling. Daily petting is a must, and is just as important as the right kind of food. It's up to the cat to decide when and how much physical contact is needed.

✔ Cats need the food that they're used to. They don't like surprises in their diet. They can be very picky until the right kind of food is found – and it certainly needn't be the most expensive kind. But from time to time you can try to introduce a little variety to the food dish. In contrast to dogs, which devour their food, cats eat at a leisurely pace.

✔ Cats need their familiar surroundings, for they have a strong sense of place. The accustomed surroundings provide security and strength. On their home turf, even gentle kittens will challenge pushy macho male cats. Every change in their living quarters that affects their sleeping or resting places meets with their disapproval. Cats are unhappy in houses where the furniture is constantly rearranged. Moving to a new house is a traumatic experience for a cat; in the ensuing weeks, it will need plenty of comforting and petting to help it get used to its new home.

✔ Cats need undivided love. They are quick to become jealous; people and

animals that are new arrivals in their sphere (such as babies, a mate, a dog, or another cat) often trigger defiance, defensiveness, or protest. The cat sees its preeminence threatened and feels neglected. It will take plenty of patience and devotion to convince the cat that it's still the focus of attention (see page 36).

What Your Cat Needs from You

In spite of the cat's great adaptability, there are some requirements that cat owners and the new cat home must offer to guarantee a harmonious partnership.

✔ Cats like niches and corners in the house where they can take refuge. The structure and setup of the house are more important than the size of the living area.

✔ Cats don't appreciate it when certain rooms are off-limits. But if you don't want to share your bed with the cat, the door to the bedroom should always be kept shut from the very beginning.

✔ Lookout points by windows provide variety in a cat's daily routine.

✔ If there are smokers in the house, cats need to have some smoke-free rooms where they can spend time.

✔ A balcony that has been made safe with a net from the pet shop and that offers a chance to do some climbing is the crowning touch to a cat's home.

✔ Indoor cats need a scratching post. Even that doesn't guarantee that the sofa and armchairs will escape without damage (see page 39).

✔ Avoid keeping houseplants that are poisonous to cats (see page 45).

✔ Set aside an hour every day for cuddling and playing. Many purebred cats also need daily grooming.

T I P

Are Indoor Cats Happy?

Many cat owners wrestle with the issue of letting their cat run free. With dogs, it's a clear-cut situation: They are runners, and they need their daily exercise. Cats also need exercise, but not to the same extent as dogs. Cats can move very fast when they need to, but in their normal routine they prefer to take things easy.

People who keep their cats indoors therefore don't need to worry because the animal is confined to the house. It's much more important to pay attention to the cat on a regular basis: Playing with a toy mouse or a little ball develops the cat's coordination and keeps it fit; in stalking it learns to be observant and use its wits. When it plays at hunting, it practices and refines its inherited techniques for catching prey, and it burns off pent-up energy (especially when it plays with the "prey").

Playing with a human provides more than an athletic and healthy feline body, for it also strengthens the partnership. For many cats the playtime with their owner is the high point of the day, and they would even leave their food for it. This means care and responsibility on the human's part: anytime the play session is neglected, the cat is disappointed. If that's repeated, it may act insulted and respond with protest.

What Does My Dream Cat Look Like?

Your cat should feel comfortable with you; it should provide you with pleasure and enrich your life. You too are capable of making compromises, but you would resist having to do without some preferred custom. In order to avoid false expectations and subsequent conflicts, you should first figure out what kind of cat is right for you: The proper choice is the first step to a harmonious partnership. If you don't have much experience with cats, you can get information from agencies and service departments of cat associations, from cat breeders, veterinarians, and cat sitters (see the Appendix, pages 62–63).

Norwegian Forest Cats: purebred beauty with the characteristic ruff.

House Cat or Purebred Cat?

Specific breeds of cat have been around for only about a hundred years. Cat breeding focuses mostly on preserving beauty and typical characteristics. There are hardly any differences in physique and behavior between purebreds and common house cats.

Purebreds: Particular kinds of fur and personality types go with certain breeds. Also, people who have a clear idea of their dream cat can avoid getting a "pig in a poke" by buying a purebred.

Common House Cats: These cats are usually cheaper to buy – and are available from shelters – and they require less care.

Kitten or Grown Cat?

Kitten: Practically no one can avoid the charm of a kitten. But the same is not true for the responsibility they represent. Kittens are ready for adoption no earlier than at the age of twelve weeks; at that point, they're no longer so fixated on their mother, and they are curious about everything. Just the same, the pain of separation from mother and siblings is very profound. In the first days, the kitten will need attention from the owner around the clock. The kitten shouldn't even be left alone during the night; it should sleep next to your bed. The little kitten tummy will hold only small amounts of food, so you will have to feed it every three hours. Thanks to special kitten chow available at pet stores, it's easy to provide the right nutrition nowadays. The young cat is not housebroken, though; it will, however, quickly learn to use the designated litter box. Reward it and pet it every time it does the right thing. The most important part of the daily schedule is sleep – up to twenty hours of it! Plenty of play and cuddling soon forge a close friendship between person and cat.

Adult Cats: With older cats it usually takes longer to achieve mutual interest and friendship. Cats

from an animal shelter have often gone through the hands of several owners, and animals that were abandoned will probably have to get over some traumatic experiences. You'll need to use lots of patience, and it will help if you have some experience with cats. Full-grown cats have some advantages: They are already housebroken and self-assured, and they don't need constant attention.

Male or Female Cat?

Female cats are reputed to be more independent, and male cats more sociable. That's sometimes true, but every animal has its individual characteristics. Its behavior with people depends on whether its needs for rest, a predictable daily routine, cuddling, food, and care are provided. During the mating season (two to three times a year), females become restless and noisy, and male cats mark their territory by spraying urine. Neutering eliminates this sexual behavior (see page 23).

Independent, self-confident, open to new experiences: every cat has its own personality.

Are You a Cat Person?

✔ Do you have experience with cats?

Yes (4 points); in my youth we had a cat (2); no (0).

✔ What do you know about the lifestyle, behavior, and needs of a cat?

I have had practical experience from owning a cat (4); I have gotten some information from books and magazines (3); not much, I'm afraid (0).

✔ Is your financial situation stable enough to afford care for a cat over fifteen or twenty years?

Yes (4); in emergencies relatives and friends would have to help with the expenses (2); that's not certain (0).

✔ A cat will change your life. Are you prepared to modify your routine for the benefit of your cat?

Yes, I'm aware of the responsibilities (4); the cat will simply have to adapt (0).

✔ The litter box will need to be cleaned regularly. Will that be a problem for you?

No, that's all part of owning a cat (4); as long as you use good kitty litter, you don't have to clean the box every day (2); someone else in the family will have to take care of this chore (0).

✔ Even clean animals like cats leave a trail behind them. Can you live with cat hair, and even some scratches on your good furniture?

Yes (4); not really, but we'll get the cat trained properly (2); no – from the outset certain rooms will be off-limits (0).

✔ Will there be any company for your cat when you have to be out of the house for a fairly long time?

Yes, we intend to get two cats (4); friends or a cat sitter will take care of the cat (3); probably not (0).

✔ Will you take your cat into account when you plan your vacations?

We wouldn't leave unless there were plans in place for the cat's care (4); we'll rely on a neighbor to take care of the cat (0).

✔ Cats eventually grow old and even sick, and then they need lots of attention and care. Are you prepared to deal with that?

Yes, we have already talked that over in detail with family and friends (4); I can't worry too much about that at this point (0).

✔ Do you intend to speak to a veterinarian about shots and a routine checkup before you get a cat?

Of course (4); that's something I'll take care of once the cat develops a problem (0).

✔ How would you react if your cat brought a mouse into the house?

I would gently lead the cat back outdoors (4); I'm scared to death of mice (0).

Add up the number of points indicated in parentheses for the answers you have chosen. (You'll find the key to the test on page 15.)

One, Two, or Several Cats?

Cats get along fine alone, but they appreciate company from time to time. Cats always form the closest bond with their reference person – even if they have other feline friends in the house. People who can spend a couple of hours every day with their little housemate will have a happy cat. That's true for working people too, who should not leave their cats alone for more than four to six hours a day and come home promptly at a specific time. Cats expect their owners to spend time with them after their return (see page 41). Things are different with solo cats that have to stay alone for longer periods of time, or whose owners return home at different times; they suffer from uncertainty about when and if the door will ever open again. That's even worse for indoor cats. People who can't modify their daily routine, but who still want a cat, should at least provide some company for the animal. The best combinations are two littermates, or a mother and son. If you get a second cat later on, the first cat will usually become jealous. You can facilitate their adapting to each other by providing attention and private space for both (sleeping places, food dishes, and litter boxes). Sometimes the adaptation is difficult, and in rare cases it may not happen at all. But usually after a few weeks the two cats become very close to each other.

How About a Cat from an Animal Shelter?

In animal shelters, people with professional knowledge and devotion take care of unloved and abandoned animals. Just the same, the animal shelter can't replace a cat's family. Take a leisurely look around your local animal shelter during visiting hours (usually on weekends). The personnel who work there will

Answer Key to Are You a Cat Person?

39–44 points: You are the ideal person for a cat! And your house will be paradise for it.

33–38 points: A cat will be happy living with you. Sometimes you tend to think of your own needs first. That's not a problem, and the cat will be able to live with it.

24–32 points: You are truly interested in providing a home for a cat. Evidently you don't yet know much about what cats need and desire. Try to see the world from time to time from the viewpoint of your cat.

less than 24 points: You're still some distance away from being a cat person. Currently only your needs are important. Unfortunately, a cat won't be happy living with you.

explain the requirements and the characteristics of the cats. For the most part, these are grown animals, since it's less common for kittens to show up at a shelter. All cats are regularly examined by a veterinarian. They are wormed, inoculated, and neutered. The purchase price covers a part of the shelter's costs for care and veterinary services. Pay close attention to the advice of the caregivers concerning feeding and handling the cat. That will make it easier for the cat to become acclimated, and it will save you aggravation and stress. If you are not yet fairly experienced in dealing with cats, you should choose only a shelter cat whose complete history is known.

PROFILES OF

Maine Coon: imposing, medium-longhaired cat. Best kept in an enclosure for outdoor exercise.

Somali: good-natured and devoted, but also temperamental and playful.

Favorite Cat Breeds

Cat breeds can be divided into four groups: longhaired, shorthaired, medium-longhaired, and Siamese and Oriental cats (single-colored Siamese relatives). There are different colors in almost all breeds.

Note: The criteria for individual breeds are established in what's known as the breed standards. They describe the best type for a breed with reference to body configuration, coat structure, color, and markings, as well as specific character traits.

Persian (photo below)

They are unmistakable: long, thick fur;

Turkish Van: playful, but very strong willed. Enjoys swimming.

large, round head with short, broad nose. Typical to the breed: the *break* or *stop* between forehead and nose. Persians are reserved and gentle, and they are very strongly attached to their owner. There are nearly two hundred fur colors and types. Persians are good indoor cats.

Persian: calm and deliberate. The coat definitely needs daily care.

PUREBRED CATS

Rag Doll: calm and composed, and fond of children. This breed was developed fairly recently.

Holy Birman: In this color variant, the white paws are hardly noticeable.

Siamese (photo at right)
Siamese are the exact opposite of Persians in nearly every respect: strong willed, lively, always in motion, with a piercing voice. The

Siamese: strong willed, demanding, always on the move, loud voice. A good choice only for experienced cat owners.

Burmese: alert, playful, and interested in everything. Likes to fetch.

light, short fur always shows some darker sections (points) on the head, legs, back, and tail. Typical of the breed: high, slender physique, blue eyes. They need lots of affection. The Balinese (see page 19) is the longhaired version of the Siamese.

Burmese (photo above)
The friendly, sociable Burmese resembles the Siamese in physique and behavior, but it is not quite as slender, and it's a bit more calm. There are ten recognized fur colors; Burma brown is typical.

Maine Coon (photo on page 16)
Very large, medium-longhaired breed (males weigh up to twenty pounds/nine kg), with broad chest and powerful legs. Originated in the state of Maine. The designation *coon* refers to the ringed pattern on the tail, reminiscent of raccoons. The cat's squeaky voice is a marked contrast to its physical size. This breed requires lots of affection and company.

Somali (photo on page 16)
Even though these cats are grouped among the medium-longhaired breeds, the Somalis' fur is relatively short and thin. The kittens are born with a short coat, and the typical Somali look develops only later. Typical of the breed are a bushy tail and long hair on the hind legs ("trousers"). Somalis come in many colors. The Somali is the longhaired relative of the Abyssinian.

Rag Doll (photo on page 17)
An American breed that is rarely seen outside the United States. The name refers to a breed characteristic: when you pick up a Rag Doll, it lets its limbs hang down limp and motionless like a stuffed doll. This is a large, vocal, medium-longhaired cat with a bushy tail that is full grown only after three years.

Holy Birman (photo on page 17)
Typical of the breed are the white "shoes" on all four paws. The body is white or cream-colored; the face mask, legs, ears, and tail have dark points (usually brown or blue).
The long, silky fur requires daily care. They are affectionate but not pushy, and they get along well with other house pets.

Abyssinian (see large photo on page 25)
Many people believe that the Abyssinian is descended from the cats of the pharaohs of northern Africa. Their appearance makes this supposition understandable: slender body, long tail, large ears, usually orange-brown short fur. Further colors include blue-gray and copper-red. Abyssinians don't take to everyone and remain reserved with strangers. The Somali (see description at left) is the longhaired version of the Abyssinian.

Turkish Angora (see illustration below, right)
The Turkish Angora is a medium-longhaired cat that, in contrast to the other medium-longhaired cats, has no insulating coat. It is devoted, lively, playful, good with children, and not as vocal as the Orientals. Turkish Angoras

From left to right: Carthusian, Turkish Angora in white, Balinese with dark points, and European Shorthair, a counterpart of the house cat.

and others that are white (and often blue-eyed) may be deaf.

Norwegian Forest
Cat (photo on page 12)
Norwegians are large cats with a medium-long, thick coat of fur and an imposing ruff. Thanks to the water-repellent fur, even long prowls in ice and snow are no problem for these powerful cats. These cats may be all one color or striped in various coat colors. They are even tempered, gentle, and peace loving; they need company and shouldn't be kept alone.

European Shorthair
(see illustration below)
In appearance, these cats resemble the typical, common house cat. The European Shorthair is a recently developed breed that has been officially recognized only since 1982, and it's not frequently encountered. It is robust and durable, and it is bred in numerous colors.

Carthusian (see illustration below, left)
The Carthusian is another name applied to the blue variant of the British Shorthair. The short coat is thick and velvety soft. Carthusians are powerful cats with a noticeably large head.

The blue eyes of the kittens later change to orange. They are friendly, easygoing, and well adjusted.

Balinese (see illustration below)
The Balinese is a longhaired variant of the Siamese, with a wedge-shaped head, large eyes, and a slender, high body. The long, silky fur, the bushy tail, and the dark points give this breed its distinctiveness. People who like the Siamese breed, but want a cat that's a little more discreet and gentle, will be happy with a Balinese.

Turkish Van (photo on page 16)
This breed originated in the Lake Van region of Turkey. These cats gladly go into the water to catch fish. They have a medium-long, soft coat and light brown spots on the forehead and ears. The tail is light brown. Because they are extremely devoted to their reference person, they are not a good choice for a family cat.

Checklist
Getting a Kitten

Here are some things to keep in mind when you get a kitten:

1 The kitten should be at least twelve weeks old.

2 Starting when the kitten is at least five weeks old, visit the mother and kitten at least two times.

3 The kitten of your choice should have a shiny coat with no bald or unkempt spots.

4 It should be lively and curious, and it should move with no perceptible lameness.

5 The eyes must be clear and sparkling, the ears clean; breathing is noiseless, the gums are pink, and the bottom is tidy.

6 It's usual for young cats to have a little bit of a belly. But a noticeable waistline or a round, distended belly can also be a sign of worms.

7 Here's how to tell the sex: In a male, the anus and sex organ are farther apart than in a female.

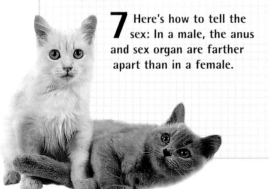

Things You Should Know Before Buying a Cat

Purchase Price. Even purebred cats don't cost an arm and a leg. Prices may vary considerably among regions, but you can expect to pay more for rare breeds and award-winning breeding stock. There is no guarantee that decorated show animals will produce championship offspring.

If you're not looking for a kitten that has an ancestral portrait gallery, you may hit pay dirt in your neighborhood or the local barnyard. Oftentimes cat owners are grateful to see their kittens go to good homes, and give them away for free. Then you'll have to take care of the checkup with the vet (initial examination, worming, and shots).

Legal Considerations. Renters are usually allowed to keep cats as long as the rental contract contains no specific clauses prohibiting pet ownership. As long as the cat is not a nuisance, a clause prohibiting ownership may not be enforceable. In some condominiums, prohibition of pet ownership is possible only by unanimous resolution by the owners. An exception is unreasonable damage caused by too many cats. Wherever you live, however, it is best to check the local laws.

Basic Equipment. The following are the things you should have on hand before the cat moves in: a bed (cat basket, basket, or box) in a quiet corner protected from draft; stable food and water dishes; a litter box; a scratching post or tree; toys; perhaps a cat door for cats that go outdoors; a comb; a brush; and some health aids (see page 23).

Costs. Pet shops offer a large selection of cat baskets in several price ranges. Food dishes made of clay or stoneware are inexpensive; good quality steel will cost more.

There are simple litter boxes made of plastic shells and luxurious toilets with roofs. You'll have to figure in some extra money for food, treats, dietary supplements, and vitamins; and don't forget visits to the vet for shots and general checkups. Neutering is another expense; you can find out how much it will cost by contacting your veterinarian or animal shelter.

The Right Choice

Getting a Kitten: Visit the cat family a minimum of two times after the kittens are at least five weeks old and before they are ready to go; take time in deciding which kitten to choose.

Buying a Purebred Cat: Learn to recognize the various breeds by visiting cat shows (check

A kitten comes to live at home: this is the start of an exciting time for human and animal.

notices in newspapers and cat magazines). There is literature available on practically every breed. Then visit two or three breeders so you can observe the cats in their familiar surroundings.

Cats from an Animal Shelter: In animal shelters you will find mostly adult cats (see page 15).

Note: Get your cat to the vet soon, especially if it doesn't have a complete shot record. Before you let it outdoors, give it time to get used to your house. Kittens shouldn't be let out before they are sixteen to eighteen weeks old.

Cat Care Made Easy

Healthy cats take care of their body and fur regularly and frequently. Obviously neglected, unkempt fur, or matted fur around the anus is therefore an indication of physical or psychological problems.

Every cat owner should help the cat with its care. Most chores don't take much time, and they require no special skills. For cats that have grown accustomed to it from youth, grooming is like petting and cuddling.

Coat Care

Use a comb and brush to remove loose hair, dirt, and any parasites on the skin or in the fur, and to untangle any matted fur.

Shorthaired cats: Comb your cat once or twice weekly with a metal comb – always in the direction of the lay of the fur – and brush it with a natural-bristle or synthetic brush.

Longhaired and Medium-longhaired Cats: Groom the fur a couple of times a week (daily with Persians)

using a broad-toothed comb and a brush. Carefully untangle matted areas of the coat by hand. At the same time, check fur and skin for injuries and changes caused by illness (such as red or bald spots, hair loss, or damage to fur). Tangles that you can't undo will have to be clipped by the vet under sedation.

Note: If you suspect that your cat has fleas, put it onto a white surface (e.g., paper or a bathtub). Fleas are difficult to detect in cat fur, but you'll see the black flea droppings when you comb them out onto the white surface.

Body Care

Eyes: Check daily for discharge in the corner of the eye; that's easy to remove with a soft, damp cloth.

Ears: Dark-colored deposits and an unpleasant smell are indications of mites. Merely dab the outer ear with a damp cloth. Never poke around inside a cat's ear with a cotton swab! Cleaning the inner ear is only for the vet.

Mouth and Teeth: In order to check the cat's throat and teeth, you have to open its mouth: Use one hand to reach around the back of the head; use the thumb and middle finger to pull upward carefully on the upper jaw while the other hand keeps the lower jaw still. A strong odor from the mouth and red or receding gums are signs of disease; normal gums are pink. With a little skill you can even get a cat used to a toothbrush. That also provides a massage for the gums.

Ready for a checkup. People who groom their cats keep them in good health.

Anal Region: A soiled or matted anal region is a sign of stomach or digestive problems such as diarrhea. Overweight cats neglect to clean their bottom because it's hard for them to reach that part of their body.

Claw Care: Claws need to be shortened when they grow too long. Your vet will show you how to do this. Important: Trim only the tips of the claws, and avoid cutting into the quick.

The Most Important Visits to the Veterinarian

Immunizations: Write the shot schedule in red on your calendar; a complete series of inoculations is essential to your cat's well-being.

The basic immunizations against the most common infectious diseases are administered between the ninth and the twelfth weeks of a cat's life. FIP immunizations are done in the sixteenth and nineteenth weeks. The vaccinations have to be reinforced yearly, usually by means of a combination shot. Before the shots, the cat should be wormed. Nowadays there are shots to prevent rabies, FIP, leukemia, cat distemper (panleukopenia), and feline respiratory disease (rhinotracheitis).

Neutering: Neutering involves removing the male cat's testicles and the female cat's ovaries. Most veterinarians recommend having a cat neutered as early as possible (around the age of six months). Neutering eliminates pregnancy and stops the sex drive. It keeps male cats from marking (spraying urine) and keeps females from coming into heat.

Neutered animals tend to wander less, and are better adjusted and more devoted.

If you don't intend to use your purebred cat for breeding purposes, you should have it neutered to avoid unwanted litters.

TIP

Health Aids for Cats

Health aids for cats facilitate convalescence and care of cats that are sick or that have recently had surgery, and they help in complying with the veterinarian's orders.

✔ Hot water bottle and a soft blanket: warmth promotes healing and is especially important after an operation so that the patient doesn't get cold.

✔ A pipette and syringe (with needle removed): for administering liquid medications and fluid nutrients in cases of loss of appetite and refusal to eat.

✔ Disinfectants: used for keeping the area of a sick animal free of microbes that cause disease. Your vet can recommend the best kinds (without iodine, phenols, and alcohol).

✔ Worm medicine: preventive treatment for worms.

✔ Thermometer: a baby thermometer from the drugstore will be useful in taking the cat's rectal temperature (normal temperature = 101.5° F / 38.6°C).

✔ Vaseline: used as a lubricant when taking a cat's temperature and for treating cracked foot pads.

✔ Cotton pads and soft fleece: useful in caring for sick animals that can't keep themselves clean.

✔ Cotton cloth: for compresses and emergency first aid.

Note: Use medications for diarrhea, and eye and ear drops only as needed and at the recommendation of a veterinarian. All medications from the medicine chest at home are unsuited for use with cats.

Parasites: Pet shops have some very effective treatments for skin and fur parasites such as fleas and ticks; these include flea collars and flea powder, and pincers for ticks. In case of massive infestation involving bald spots or apathetic behavior, the animal needs the care of a veterinarian.

Bite Wounds: They may look harmless, but bite wounds often become infected. If your cat sustains this type of injury, always take it to a vet as a precaution.

Poisoning: If your cat ingests dangerous substances such as cleaning solutions or pills, the packaging or list of ingredients will indicate lifesaving first-aid measures.

Note: Cats are tough, and they sometimes conceal serious illnesses for a long time. So be alert to small changes in your cat's behavior. Write down everything you observe so that the doctor can have a complete picture of what's going on.

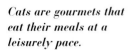

Cats are gourmets that eat their meals at a leisurely pace.

The Ten-Point Feeding Program for Cats

Commercially prepared foods contain everything that a cat needs to remain healthy. At pet shops there are also special foods available for young, pregnant, elderly, ill, and overweight animals.

1. Never serve the food directly from the refrigerator. Cat food should be at least room temperature.

2. Keep the daily serving sizes within the manufacturer's recommendations.

3. Feed the cat at predictable times during the day. Grown cats can be fed up to twice a day, older cats three times, and young cats every three to four hours.

4. Cats are deliberate eaters. They don't "wolf" their food down, but pause in the process. Leave the bowl in place for thirty to forty-five minutes before you clean up the leftovers.

5. Fresh water at room temperature should always be available, especially when the cat is given dry food.

6. Milk is a food, and it's no substitute for drinking water. The lactose component in milk produces diarrhea in many cats. Pet shops sell special cat milk.

7. Human food is taboo for cats. If you feed your cat in the morning and evening before eating your own meals, the cat won't be inclined to beg at the table.

8. Bones, spicy food, sweets, and dog food are not for cats. They will lead to deficiency diseases and other illness.

9. Even cats that catch mice need normal portions of food.

10. After every meal the cat should have an opportunity to do some grooming and take a snooze.

Ten Golden Rules for
Keeping a Cat

1 Cats like predictable schedules: prompt feeding, punctual times for cuddling, being let out at predictable times, and siestas at the same time of day.

2 Noise and rapid movements are an abomination to cats. They will tend to slink away or react defensively or aggressively.

3 Commands and reproaches are taken by cats as rejection. They will cooperate only at their own initiative. It's best if you can arouse their natural curiosity and playfulness.

4 If a cat feels slighted, as when a baby gets more attention, it is quick to take offense and react in protest (see page 36).

5 Cats are creatures of habit. They react with skepticism or rejection to changes in food, the house, or their territory, and to unfamiliar people and new house pets.

6 Cats like to play as long as they live. Playing keeps them physically fit and healthy. Give your cat the opportunity to keep itself busy, and set aside at least an hour a day to play with it.

7 Cats form a close bond with their humans. Cuddling, petting, and gentle physical contact are important signs of friendship.

8 Cats need long periods of rest and sleep. A cat that is frequently disturbed in its sleep will become susceptible to illness.

9 The house is the cat's territory. Closed doors interfere with inspecting its domain. The cat will have to get used to any places that are off limits while it's young.

10 It will take just a minute every day to check your cat's health: fur, eyes, mouth, teeth, and digestion (see page 22).

New Life with a Cat

Whether family or singles, working people or senior citizens, country or city people, home-owners or condominium dwellers, people who enter into a partnership with a cat take on responsibilities and have to include their needs when making decisions, and they have to be ready to compromise in daily living. Mere goodwill is not enough, and it's only in concrete situations that it becomes evident whether the willingness to work together amounts to anything more than lip service. And you have to remember that your union with the cat may last fifteen or twenty years.

Things You Must Do Every Day

✔ Feed adult cats once or twice, older animals (age ten and up) three times, kittens every three to four hours.
✔ Provide fresh drinking water.
✔ Wash the dishes with hot water.
✔ Replace all or part of the kitty litter and check the droppings for consistency and color.
✔ Check eyes, nose, and ears for discharge or uncleanliness.

✔ Comb and brush longhaired cats.
✔ Check cats that go outdoors for fleas and ticks.
✔ Pet and play with the cat.

Once a Week

✔ Buy canned food.
✔ Clean up resting and sleeping areas.
✔ Remove cat hair from carpets, sofa, and chairs.
✔ Coat care for shorthaired breeds.
✔ Check coat of indoor cats.
✔ Check claws.
✔ Thorough cleaning of litter box with hot water, and if necessary, an environmentally safe cleanser.
✔ Change and wash blankets and pillows from cat bed and resting place.

Once a Month

✔ Buy dry food and vitamin and mineral supplements.

Every Three to Four Months

✔ Worm cats that are allowed outside.

Once or Twice a Year

✔ Worm indoor cats.
✔ Go for a routine checkup at the vet's.
✔ Get booster shots.

As Necessary

✔ Trim claws.
✔ Flea and tick collar.

Cats can't get to birds in a cat-proof bird house.

Dominance display: Arching the back and raising the hackles are meant to impress the rival.

Taking Care of Kittens

Kittens are ready to go live with you at the age of about twelve weeks. That's a traumatic experience for the kitten: All of a sudden there are no more mother and siblings, and the surroundings and the people are all strange. The kitten feels abandoned and frightened.

✔ During the first four weeks, do your best to avoid leaving the kitten alone.

✔ The first nights the kitten should sleep by your bed. A clock wrapped in a blanket in the cat bed, or soft background music can have a soothing effect. Be understanding if at first you are frequently awakened in the night by pitiful meowing.

✔ Set up a schedule with the vet for completing the basic immunizations.

✔ Feed smaller portions of kitten food from the pet shop several times a day.

✔ Regularly massage the kitten's tummy to stimulate digestion.

✔ Kittens need an inordinate amount of sleep. Take care not to disturb it.

✔ Get the kitten used to the litter box; in the first few days, place it inside the box. Also, reward the cat when it does its business properly. From the very start, keep the litter box in a fixed location.

Play and Activities

Cats are among the few animals that like to play throughout their lives and sharpen their skills for stalking and catching prey. Even older cats can be motivated to play. Set aside playtime every day! Whether the game involves playing with a Ping-Pong ball or a toy on a string, searching for a stuffed mouse, or attacking playfully, it's essential that the human take part. If the cat has to stay alone, it needs something to do, such as cardboard boxes to hide in, a scratching post for climbing and sharpening its claws, cat grass to chew, a toy mouse, and balls to play with. It's also important to have a place at the window where the cat can watch the exciting world outside and forget that it's alone.

Note: If your cat has to spend a lot of time alone each day, it's a good idea to have a second cat for company. But even then the cats shouldn't be left alone more than six hours a day. The daily playtime together is important even when you have two cats.

Rubbing against your legs – a gesture of the cat's affection for people it likes.

A DREAM CAT FOR THE FAMILY

Cats react sensitively to the character and the voices of the people in their surroundings. They have an individual relationship with different people. When their basic needs are met, they are the perfect partners for all family members, from granddad to toddler.

How Will Family Life Be Different?

Everything revolves around the cat. Cats are self-assured and want to be the center of everything. That applies even to animals that are at first insecure and shy in strange surroundings. Oftentimes, once the inhibitions are overcome, scaredy-cats turn into saucy but lovable domestic tyrants. Dogs are relegated to a place in the family pack, but cats insist on taking over the nicest armchair. With dogs you address problems and misunderstandings with clear commands, as long as the requisite training is in place. But cats that feel misunderstood by their people and behave defiantly often require persuasion to get them to cooperate or to stop sulking.

Cats need time and closeness. The family is best suited to meeting these requirements. If the chores are shared among all family members, perhaps in revolving fashion, the cat will always have what it needs, and no one will grumble about having too much to do: filling the food and water dishes, cleaning the dishes, buying food, cleaning the litter box,

tidying up the resting and sleeping places, grooming, and taking the cat to the vet's. If everyone helps take care of the cat, it will show its appreciation with love and affection.

Cats give the family a new focal point. This becomes clear even if the daily schedule and hustle and bustle have so far left little time for one another; with a cat in the house, people get back together for dinner and fun playtimes. And they resume talking about their great and minor experiences, their wishes, dreams, and concerns. Sometimes people even establish new priorities: Previously the business luncheon and the tennis game were essential, and now it's nice to have a reason to come home early – partly because there's a cat waiting, but also because now the whole family is there more often. Cats foster togetherness; they promote gentle voices and movements, and they help us to see things in a more positive light. The reason for that is that cats react positively and open-mindedly to their surroundings.

The Road to Finding a Family Cat

Even if everyone in the family is excited about the cat, you still shouldn't be blind to the compromises that will be required in living with this new family member. Ideally the family will talk things over and come to an understanding before the cat moves in so that little problems don't grow into big ones.

Private Space: The cat will need its own private space, and so will every family member. Some senior citizens may find a lively kitten to be an annoyance if the children play with it and turn the house upside down. Grandma and Grandpa have a right to their peace and quiet. It's fine if some rooms are off-limits to the cat. **Important Note**: Lay down the rules before the cat moves in, because it will be much harder to do so later on.

Division of Labor: Everyone wants to have a cat, and everyone promises to take care of it. But duties like the daily cleaning of the litter box often spoil the enthusiasm in a hurry. In the final analysis, one family member often ends up taking on the responsibilities of the others. A weekly or monthly schedule of duties can keep that from happening. The chores are rotated regularly, and everyone gets a chance to be at the head of the line.

Scheduling: In contrast to a cat owned by a single person, a family cat is rarely alone. Just the same, it shouldn't be assumed that someone will always be in the house. Work hours and school can't be put off, but goodwill and coordination can often work wonders. Ideally, the schedule can be coordinated with the division of labor.

Sources of Danger: Especially with little kittens, which don't have much experience in life and are very curious, you have to eliminate or reduce sources of danger such as an open washing machine – since holes have a magical attraction for cats – and hot burners. (For further Sources of Danger, see page 45.)

A Cat-Friendly House: Cats value order and supervision. Everything should be in its accustomed place; continual rearranging of furniture will result in protest and behavior problems. A house that's set up properly for cats will offer outlooks at windows, with wide windowsills, places to lie down, a cat bed, a litter box, a scratching post, a climbing rope, cat grass, toys, and boxes for hiding and playing.

First examination: the cat carefully inspects the new family member.

Purebred Cats for the Family

Purebred cats that are suitable for a family should be well adjusted, as calm and friendly as possible, and active and playful. Children can sometimes play rough with the cat and can be noisy; the cat must be physically healthy, and it shouldn't hide under the sofa in fear at every noise.

Breed	Type	Temperament	Characteristics
Abyssinian	slender, robust shorthaired cat	intelligent, active, and very playful	demanding, likes to climb, needs lots of attention, coat is easy to care for
British Shorthair	compact shorthaired cat, powerful legs, many varieties	well adjusted and friendly	adult males are much larger than females; blue variant: Carthusian
Burmese	muscular shorthaired cat	alert, playful	wide variety of colors, very sociable
European Shorthair	looks like a normal house cat	well adjusted, friendly, confident	robust, healthy, easy to care for, strong hunting instinct
Holy Birman	medium-longhaired cat with white "gloves"	pleasant, gentle, and very people oriented	ideal cat for a family
Carthusian	powerful shorthaired breed with thick, blue-gray fur	calm, sedate, and friendly	only one permissible coat color; good with children, easy to care for
Maine Coon	imposing and robust medium-longhaired cat	friendly but independent	late developer, needs to go outdoors, best if it has a companion
Norwegian Forest Cat	large and powerful medium-longhaired cat	curious, active, and friendly	like the Maine Coon, best to have a companion
Rag Doll	large medium-longhaired cat	very calm, friendly, and sociable	late developer, good with children, ideal family cat
Turkish Angora	slender medium-longhaired cat	lively, playful, devoted, curious	easier grooming than with other longhaired breeds; needs outdoor exercise

All shorthaired breeds are easy to care for. The medium-longhaired cats with a silky coat like the Angoras are much less work than longhaired breeds like the Persians.

Note: Individual differences in the nature of cats (such as devotion, curiosity, playfulness) can be greater than the differences among separate breeds.

CAT CARE DURING VACATION

Cats usually don't care to travel. Even on short trips, many cats are panic-stricken in a car, and longer trips can be agonizing for both animal and humans. Most cats stay home and need to have someone look after them who can be responsible not only for the animals' care, but also for their psychological well-being. Cats are best off in the hands of a cat sitter; check your phone book. Cat sitters have experience in dealing with cats, and they will come to the house. The animal stays in its familiar surroundings, and that's an advantage compared with a boarding kennel. As an alternative, you can call on relatives, friends, or neighbors who are friendly with the cat to come and feed it, pet it, and play with it. For emergencies, you should leave your vacation address and telephone number, plus the veterinarian's phone number.

Note: Even after receiving perfect care, many cats act stand-offish and offended when their humans return. Don't worry; an extra session of cuddling will bring everything back to normal.

Children and Cats

Cats are perpetual children. On the one hand, it's part of a cat's nature to keep fit and hone its hunting instincts by playing, and on the other, in partnership with humans, the cat takes on the status of an infant that will need care and attention for its entire life. Playfulness, curiosity, and love of people predestined the cat for its role as the ideal partner for children. In order for the dream relationship to function properly, children have to learn a few things about dealing with their house pet:

✔ Help your child learn about the behavior and needs of the cat. Children have to understand that cats are not toys, and they have to accept that their own desires will not always be satisfied or come first in dealing with a cat.

✔ Cats must not be disturbed when they are sleeping, eating, or using the litter box.

✔ Young cats are not yet accustomed to wild games with children. In addition, they need lots of rest. Constant disturbances during sleep will harm their healthy development.

✔ Explain to your child that cats are sensitive creatures that don't like noise and violent movement.

✔ Show your child how to pet the cat: how and where to pet it, how to tell when the cat wants to cuddle, and how it shows when it's not in the mood.

✔ Make it clear from the beginning what is not permitted: touching the cat's eyes or ears, rubbing against the lay of the fur, and fondling the cat on its belly; many cats fend that off using their claws.

✔ Little children shouldn't play with a cat without supervision. In the excitement of the game, they often become impulsive and lose

Childhood happiness with a cat: playing together is twice the fun.

control. If an otherwise patient cat is grabbed roughly or is hit, it may react by spitting, scratching, or biting.

✔ When cats use their paw to reach for a ball or a piece of string, they often use their claws. In such games, children should keep their distance, or at least hold the toy in a way that allows them to keep from being scratched.

✔ Teach your child to hold the cat properly: One hand supports the cat's hind end and the other supports the side. Smaller children are not yet ready to do this.

✔ Children can take over some of the re-sponsibility and duties associated with their four-legged friend – feeding, grooming, and cleaning the litter box, for example. Often they will gladly assume these duties and be proud to have the new responsibility.

Older children, starting with age ten, usually respond to the demands of ownership: They want their *own* cat. That means that they will take over all the duties, except for visits to the veterinarian. Of course that doesn't relieve the adults from regular supervision.

Cats and Babies

A baby arrives. Understandably, the infant is now the focus of attention. Everything centers on the baby. The cat feels neglected, is jealous, and protests in its own way (e.g., uncleanliness, avoiding people all day, aggressive behavior toward the child). You can prevent all of that. From the very first day, make enough time for your cat. Under no circumstances should you curtail the attention you devote to it. Carefully let the cat make the acquaintance of the new family member: Pet the cat in the baby's presence and let the cat sniff the infant. But even after the cat has accepted the increase in the size of the family, the cat and baby should not be left together unsupervised.

How Dangerous Is Toxoplasmosis?

Toxoplasmosis is an infectious disease that can be communicated from cats to humans. Cats become infected by eating mice or raw meat. Often the symptoms are hard to recognize. People can become infected from cat droppings. Most people have already become exposed to toxoplasmosis without realizing it and have built up the appropriate antibodies. Pregnant women who don't have the antibodies face a heightened risk; gynecologists have a test for this. Expectant mothers shouldn't let a cat lick them and should not clean the litter box.

Happiness, Sorrow, and Pain

Cats are not just partners for play and cuddling. They have their own life. That includes birth, illness, and death. Children and young people have to be made aware of these stations in a cat's life. Being present when a cat gives birth, caring for sick or injured cats, and closeness and comfort in the last hours of their life require strength and willpower – even for adults. This togetherness is part of the bond that exists between human and pet. In retrospect, most people who in their youth have witnessed sorrow, pain, or the birth of a cat see that as an important and enriching experience.

Cats Foster Independence

There are many studies and analyses that are concerned with the relationship between children and pets. One area of agreement in all these studies is that children who grow up with pets become independent earlier in life; they are in a better position to assume responsibility than children of the same age who have not had animals. Meeting the requirements and the duties that an animal imposes also strengthens understanding and a social consciousness in dealing with family, friends, schoolmates, teachers, and other important people. Among all house pets, cats place the clearest and most lasting demands on people, in part as a result of their untamed personality that is not always prepared to compromise. It offers the ideal means for training a child in responsibility and independence – unconsciously, playfully, and therefore successfully. Anyone who has spent happy years as a child with a cat regrets not having its company and closeness later on.

When Cats Grow Old

Provide a warm, protected, and undisturbed sleeping place for your older cat. Continue devoting time to it for petting and cuddling. Spread the meals out over three to four feedings, and give it lighter food designed for older cats. Take good care of it by checking its coat, feeling its body for lumps, and checking the contents of the litter box. You should take it to the vet at least twice a year. If necessary, the vet can prescribe supplements to maintain the cat's vitality.

The first symptoms of aging, starting around age ten, may be scarcely noticeable:

✔ Older cats have a heightened need for sleep and warmth. In order to stock up on warmth, they may even choose to lie down in an uncomfortable place, such as on the grate of a heat register.

✔ They neglect the regular inspection of their territory. The tone and suppleness of their body decline, and the morning prowl is often eliminated.

✔ Many older cats act ungraciously if their siesta is interrupted.

✔ Playfulness wanes. Many times older cats take less pleasure in playing because of reduced ability to jump and react, plus pain in their joints.

✔ Cats are generally picky at the food dish. This characteristic becomes more pronounced as they grow older. If the cat also loses its appetite, there can be complications. Special food for older cats that's available at pet stores often helps.

Older cats don't prowl as often and prefer to get back into the warm house.

If your cat experiences tooth problems such as loss, you should stop feeding it hard (dry) food.

✔ At advanced ages, your cat may be affected by arthritis and digestive sluggishness. But even in old age, problems with kidneys, liver, and gastric glands are rare in properly nourished cats.

✔ Decreases in suppleness make it harder for the cat to groom its fur and body. The hind end may become matted, and the fur unkempt. In such cases, you will have to take over part of the cleaning duties.

✔ Older cats seek physical contact with their people more frequently.

✔ Oftentimes vision and hearing decline. Then the cat doesn't journey far from home and is quick to return to its accustomed surroundings.

When Cats Cause Problems

Anytime your cat behaves other than as it should, that's a warning and an alarm. The cat is communicating clearly that it's not happy with its living conditions. Most problems with cats are psychological in origin. But changes in behavior can also be caused by illness and pain. Every attempt to eliminate unwanted behavior should be based on a checkup by the veterinarian. If there are no physical symptoms, you need to take a critical look at the cat's environment.

Uncleanliness: This is a cat's most common form of protest. The misdeed can be directed at various places in the house, such as the carpet or a bed, instead of the litter box.

Frequently alone and bored, cats will do stupid things.

Causes: A dirty litter box; litter box in the wrong location; inappropriate litter; use of highly scented cleaning agents; disturbances while the cat is using the litter box; the scent of sex partners; jealousy of a baby, the reference person's new mate, or a new house pet; inadequate attention; and being left alone too often.

Cure: Clean the litter box thoroughly, change its location, and change the litter or cleanser. Also cover the affected areas with plastic wrap to discourage the cat.

If the cause is jealousy or loneliness, devote more time and affection to the cat.

Note: Lack of cleanliness can also have physical causes, such as kidney and bladder problems or parasites in the digestive system. So the first step should always be a consultation with the veterinarian.

Refusal to Eat: The cat doesn't touch its food for a fairly long time.

Causes: Fear of separation and sorrow, when the trusted partner, whether human or animal, is not there because of vacation, illness, or death; change of food or food brand, because cats react sensitively to ingredients and flavor enhancers; anxiety over the presence of another, new animal in the house.

Possible causes of illness: Problems with teeth, tartar, or gums.

Cure: More attention, accustomed food, separate food dishes.

Excessive Food Consumption: The cat eats an inordinate amount and always wants more.

Causes: Worms or metabolic disease such as diabetes or hormonal imbalance. In the case of worms, the cat will lose weight despite continuous food intake. Gluttony and greed can also be caused by the presence of another, new house pet.

Cure: Treatment by a veterinarian. For gluttony, feed animals separately, stick to accustomed serving sizes, and avoid treats and between-meals snacks.

Defiance and Aggressiveness: The cat doesn't respond to attention, draws back, stays away for long periods of time, or spits and scratches.

Causes: Jealousy; irregular daily routine on the part of the owner; loneliness; curtailing of accustomed rights such as sleeping on the bed; or moving to a different house.

Cure: Plenty of attention, stable times for feeding and affection, diversion through play.

Self-destructive Behavior: The cat damages its fur and skin through continual licking, scratching, and chewing. First determine whether there are physical causes such as digestive problems, parasites in the hair or skin, or injuries.

Psychological causes: Nervousness, conflict, and insecurity in hopeless or worrisome situations. This is typical for cats that are oppressed by another domineering cat and with no means of retreat. This also occurs in cats that are continually disciplined or even beaten by their owner.

Cure: Immediately change the situation that is causing the anxiety.

Roaming: Non-neutered male cats in particular often disappear for long periods.

Cause: Patrolling and defending territorial borders against rivals; searching for sex partners. Often cats that roam have attractive "support bases" where they can get treats and petting.

Cure: Neutering makes cats more domestic and attached. Ask the neighbors to stop feeding the cat.

"I'm not talking to you anymore!" Offended cats often turn their backs to people.

Can Cats Be Trained?

Dogs are obedient servants; cats are self-willed, untrainable loners: that's the old cliché. Cats are not pack animals; they don't rely on the help and judgment of others, but rather decide for themselves what's important to them. This is exactly the basis on which training cats operates: commands are useless, and what counts are opportunities to cooperate. Cats will cooperate only when they have the motivation. So you have to make use of the cats' specific preferences: They like to be the focus of attention, to feel warmth, and to be spoiled with treats and petting. They don't like unpleasantness in the form of noise, cold, commotion, and bright light.

Note: Attempts to train your cat will be effective only when it is attentive and ready. The cat will be a poor pupil if it is roused from sleep.

Preparation for being left alone: All cats that are left alone come up with dumb ideas when they are frustrated and bored. There's no excuse for gnawed flowers, shredded curtains, scratched doors and furniture, or broken vases. The cure involves providing stimulation and things for the cat to do. Give the cat opportunities to play, climb, and explore: a stuffed mouse, a ball, a climbing rope and tree, boxes and cartons, a lookout at the window, and music. A second cat may even add some life.

Curtailing aggressiveness: Many cats don't know the boundary between playful and serious; they bite people and attack with their claws. *The Cure:* thwart the attacks with a water pistol, and simultaneously divert the cat's overflowing energy to a prey animal (a stuffed mouse). But even excessively timid cats will try to defend themselves through aggressiveness. That will require careful attempts to build trust. Until that time, avoid situations in which the cat reacts aggressively.

Protecting houseplants: Cat grass from a pet shop should be in every cat's home. That

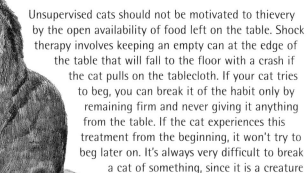

Opportunity Makes a Thief

Unsupervised cats should not be motivated to thievery by the open availability of food left on the table. Shock therapy involves keeping an empty can at the edge of the table that will fall to the floor with a crash if the cat pulls on the tablecloth. If your cat tries to beg, you can break it of the habit only by remaining firm and never giving it anything from the table. If the cat experiences this treatment from the beginning, it won't try to beg later on. It's always very difficult to break a cat of something, since it is a creature of habit.

It may also prove helpful to feed the cat before you sit down to your own meal.

This mustn't become a habit; immediately pick the cat up and put it by the scratching post.

strong plastic wrap to make them as inaccessible as possible. You might even temporarily put the food dish right next to the place, since cats don't like it when their eating area and toilet are side by side. Provide different types of litter in the litter box, and even change the location if necessary, so that the cat has more protection from drafts and unwelcome observers. Always clean the litter box with unscented cleansers. Exchange the litter box for a larger one if it's too small for the cat to turn around in and settle. Hooded litter boxes may build up odors that keep sensitive cats away.

Getting a cat to scratch in the right places: Here's how to teach your cat to use the scratching post: At every attempt to sharpen its claws on the furniture or armchairs, place the cat at its scratching post. If you rub catnip on the scratching post right from the beginning, your cat will surely take to it.

will almost always spare the houseplants. Repulse unreasonable plant nibblers with a water pistol. Cover fresh potting soil in flowerpots with stones or twigs so that it doesn't get converted to a litter box.

Away with housebreaking problems! Uncleanliness can have many causes (see pages 36–37). The cure involves making the problem area unattractive to the cat, and the litter box more appealing. Clean up the affected areas, then cover them with

Caught red-handed: you can stop plant nibblers by using a water sprayer.

CATS AND SINGLE PEOPLE – A DREAM DUO

Cats are independent creatures, but they form closer bonds with people than they do with other cats. Here's another plus to this partnership: mutual respect, a search for harmony, and longing for affection. This can be experienced more intensely in the relationship between cats and single people than in a family setting.

What's So Special About Cats and Single People?

Within a family, there are people the cat regards with reservation or even indifference, and others it clearly likes. But even this special bond of friendship can't be measured with the love, devotion, and attention that a cat brings to its single owner. For a single person's cat, the world revolves around the person: It willingly adjusts to the human's daily routine, accepts the smoke-filled room and the constant stream of music, and waits for hours at the window to see the owner come home. Of course a single person's cat makes contact with its owner's friends and acquaintances, and if it runs free, it meets other cats. But the bond with the two-legged partner is by far the strongest. The reason is simple: The relationship is very clear, and the cat always comes first, in contrast to the situation in a family.

The warmth, trust, and dependability that a person who lives alone experiences through a cat can provide calm and equanimity, and they often dispel tension and worry. The four-legged friend can open the door to more positive thoughts and new feelings, and that in turn leads to more positive relationships with other people.

But in order to create a harmonious partnership between a single person and a cat, the human has to keep two points in mind that are essential to the dream duo: dependability and order. The cat will almost always adapt to the daily routine of the person, but then it also relies on its remaining consistent. The greatest trial for a single person's cat is a disorganized owner who can't manage time and comes home at unpredictable hours. In the relationship between a single person and a cat, a predictable routine takes the highest priority: established feeding times, dependable observance of cuddling and play sessions, and a reliable return from work.

In all other areas of togetherness, the cat shows an astonishing willingness to compromise.

Cats and single people – two beings that belong to each other and tackle everything together.

TIP

Vacation Care

A cat sitter comes to your house to care for your cat. Usually this person is a cat owner and knows what cats want. Set up a time before your vacation so that the cat sitter and the cat can get to know each other. Plan to have plenty of food and litter on hand; post notes indicating feeding times, your vacation address, the address and phone number of the veterinary clinic, and the cat's habits. Include the shot record and tattoo or computer chip number (if applicable). Set up a plan involving a second caretaker in case the cat sitter can't follow through for some reason. During the vacation time, cats that normally go outside should be kept indoors. You can get addresses of cat sitters from animal shelters and cat associations (see Addresses, page 62).

The Cure for Loneliness

More and more people are living alone. Many of them do so not by choice, but rather for professional or private reasons. In spite of all their contacts, travel, sports, and other leisure activities, when they go back home they are alone. Understandably, many single people use their home only as a support base and are out as often as possible. But that has to change when a cat is taken on as a housemate. The knowledge that a lovable creature is waiting for them at home has forced many workaholics who once regarded the office as the center of operations to mend their ways. In contrast to family life, where duties and care for the animal family member can be divided up, a single person's cat keeps the owner in the position of responsibility. Many may lament, "I'll never have another evening to myself!" But if you dig a little deeper, it becomes clear that they wouldn't exchange that obligation for anything in the world. And what's more, over time, many singles and their cats develop their own rituals and ways of relating to each other that outsiders can scarcely comprehend. For example, they may both go to bed at the same time, and the cat may spend the night on the pillow. They may read the paper together at the kitchen table, or regularly watch an animal show on television. The cat may have reserved seating on the owner's shoulder, where it rides while the person takes long walks . . . the list could go on and on. Many times it happens that another person is regarded as a troublemaker, for it is difficult for that person to identify with the intimate silliness that exists between human and animal.

Searching for treats: It's important for cats that are left alone to have something to do.

Diary of a Single Person's Cat

A single person's cat doesn't just take the day as it comes. It has a fixed schedule with lots of appointments: inspecting the house and yard, taking a nap, playing, and eating meals. Activities with the owner are particularly important, and they are marked in red on the cat's daily planner.

Time	Activity
7:00	Wait until owner wakes up. Poke with paw to prevent oversleeping.
7:20	Oversee filling of food dish and rub head on owner's legs as a way of thanks.
7:45	When people eat, they still have one hand free for petting!
8:20	Stand in front of door and leave owner for a moment.
8:30	Quick wash of face and body, and earn a little snack.
9:30	Set out into territory; friendly meeting with neighbor's cat.
10:00	Successful hunt at mouse hole; call off subsequent bird hunt in tree.
10:35	Return to the house, deposit mouse in cellar.
11:00	Watch mailperson and a roaming poodle from the window.
11:30	Lengthy mid-day rest.
1:00	Inspection tour through house; discover two forgotten Ping-Pong balls in living room closet and play with them for fifteen minutes.
1:30	Thorough grooming to clean off the dirt picked up in the visit to the cellar.
2:30	Wait at the door for owner. Rambunctious greeting.
3:00	Help owner with work at desk.
5:30	Watch dinner preparation. Get treat in recognition of exemplary refraining from begging.
7:00	The high point of the day: play and cuddling with owner.
8:00	Watch an animal program on the television with owner.
10:00	Last patrol through house before going to bed.
10:30	Unsuccessful attempt to sneak into master's bed. Nod off in cat bed.

Many cats that belong to single people are used to being alone from time to time, and they usually make it through their owner's vacation all right. But with their independence of mind they often pose problems for the caregiver. And the owner often fosters that independence, even without knowing it, by becoming jealous whenever someone else gets affection from the cat. The owner is also the only person who can read the cat's desires in its eyes. And that's as it should be: The special thing about the partnership between cat and single person is the totally personal, unchangeable relationship. That's what makes the two of them the dream duo.

The Right Setup for a Single Person's Cat

Of course a single person's home has to include the necessary basic supplies for the cat: cat bed, litter box, food and water dishes, and a scratching post. But because cats that belong to single people are often left alone, the home needs to be set up properly: It has to offer plenty of variety and things to do, and there should be as few dangers as possible (see next page).

Things that make cats happy:

✔ The cat should have several types of shelter available in the home and be able to choose among various temperature ranges.

✔ There should be lookout places by the windows so the cat can participate in life outside the house; it will need a place to sit on the windowsill, so plants will have to be removed. Ideally the windowsill can be widened so that the cat can lie down; you can get special attachments for this in pet shops.

✔ A balcony that's made safe with cat netting from the pet shop allows the cat to get some fresh air and sun even when the owner is away.

✔ Possibilities for sports and play include toys (stuffed mice, balls, strings, tactile and exploration games, boxes to hide in and chew, hemp ropes to climb). But be careful with the traditional ball of yarn: The cat will quickly sink its claws into the strands and get tangled up, and it won't be able to get free without help. Regular activity keeps the cat from becoming bored, keeps it physically fit, and prevents it from using its energy to the detriment of the carpet, sofa, curtains, or furniture.

✔ Cat grass provides indoor cats with necessary greens; the grass facilitates elimination of the hair swallowed while grooming. Even cats that go outdoors and have access to grass should have cat grass. It generally keeps them from nibbling the houseplants. Pet shops sell packets of special cat grass seeds. After watering, the grass grows in a few days. Cats also like parsley, sage, and catnip.

✔ Cats like elevated sleeping places. In the outdoors, they use those perches to watch what goes on in their territory. In the house cats likewise prefer strategic spots on the top shelf of a bookcase or on a high piece of furniture. You can facilitate access to these spots by providing climbing aids, footholds, and jumping places.

A single person's cat is always ready to play a game for two.

Dangers in the House

✔ Washing machines: Cats are curious and like to investigate every dark hole. Soft laundry in the washing machine is an invitation to take a nap; a lack of observation on the owner's part could lead to a catastrophe!

✔ Open flame and hot burners: Cats sometimes perceive heat and fire only after it's too late. As long as burners or stove top are in use, the cat needs to be supervised or kept out of the kitchen altogether. Watch out for residual heat once the burners are turned off. The same applies to open flames in the fireplace or on candles. Cats also need to be kept away from boiling water and hot foods.

Siesta for a single person's cat: There's plenty of time for a snooze while the master is away at work.

✔ Poisonous plants: There's no place in a cat's house for poinsettia, Christmas rose, azalea, or dieffenbachia. When you buy a houseplant, find out whether it's toxic to cats. If the cat is allowed into the yard, there should be no rhododendron or oleander.

✔ Dangerous substances: alcohol, cleansers, disinfectants, insecticides, and rat poison are highly poisonous to cats. Even medications need to be kept locked away.

Purebred Cats for Single People

Cats for single people are subject to some special requirements: They should be devoted and people oriented, calm and well adjusted, but also independent and confident. They should be attentive partners for their human, but able to keep themselves occupied while the owner is away. The following chart presents some purebred cats that have these characteristics.

Name	Type	Temperament	Special Traits
British Shorthair	compact, stocky, round face	well adjusted and very sociable	equally playful and affectionate
Burmese**	muscular shorthaired cat	very intelligent, eager learner, great with children	likes all kinds of games, fetches almost like a dog
European Shorthair	resembles a normal house cat in every way	well adjusted and friendly	well adjusted, friendly, always on the go
Exotic Shorthair	cross between Persian and American Shorthair	reserved, quiet, not overly active	velvety fur, easy to care for, "doll" face
Carthusian	powerful shorthaired breed with thick, blue-gray fur	friendly and calm (like a teddy bear)	easy to care for, confident partner for a single person
Maine Coon*	very imposing, robust medium-longhaired cat	sociable, but also independent	obedient, possible to walk on a leash
Norwegian Forest Cat*	medium to large sized medium-longhaired cat	sociable and easygoing	needs to be kept busy; should not be kept singly
Persian	longhaired cat with thick fur	calm, doesn't need much exercise	typical indoor cat, daily fur care required
Rag Doll	large, medium-longhaired cat	gentle and patient	late bloomer (full grown only at age three or four)
Somali	soft, medium-length fur, expressive face	temperamental yet gentle	extremely devoted, good indoor cat

*Maine Coon, Norwegian Forest Cat: These cats should be allowed outdoors on the porch, in an enclosure, or in a fenced yard.
**Burmese: Not ideally suited to single people who are away from the house more than three hours a day.
Note: Individual personality differences (e.g., devotedness, curiosity, and playfulness) can be greater than the differences among breeds.

✔ Tip-out windows: These windows pose a life-threatening danger to cats. Animals that try to squeeze out through the narrow crack in a window and get hung up can't free themselves. Keep all windows closed that are accessible to the cat when it has to stay alone in the house. As an alternative, you may be able to get a window guard from a pet shop.

✔ Further sources of danger include plugged-in irons, plastic bags (danger of suffocation), unwatched and freely accessible foods, needles, knives, and scissors.

Two Cats in the House: Who Gets Along with Whom?

The companionship of a second cat is the most effective way to provide variety to a cat that has to spend several hours alone every day. But many cat owners try to avoid getting a second cat by claiming, "They'll never get along!" and "It will be too stressful!" The first few days probably won't be trouble free, but after a while the old and the new cats will become the best of friends.

The right combinations: A female cat (old) and a young neutered male cat (the new arrival), or a neutered male cat (old) and a young animal (new). Female cats are less placid than males. Problems are more common with two adult female cats. The best combination is two young animals from the same litter (ideally, a female and a male).

After some initial raising of the hackles in the presence of a young animal, senior cats often discover how fit and supple they still are.

Acclimating the second cat: After the arrival of the second cat, the animals should at first only hear and smell each other. The new cat should be in a different room, where it can get used to the new surroundings and people. Once the wrinkles are smoothed out, the cats can get to know each other – at first only under supervision.

In a household with two cats, the owner needn't suffer any pangs of conscience for coming home late once in a while. The three-way relationship in no way diminishes the affection between cats and human. And the expense caused by a second cat is negligible: some basic equipment (bed, dishes, litter box) and a small personal space for sleeping and resting places. You'll incur some additional costs for food and visits to the veterinarian.

The human is pulled carefully but persistently from the dream world into the cat world.

Activities for Single People's Cats

The daily routine of a house cat contains many hours of absolute inactivity, and others that are filled with excitement and alertness. In wild cats, prowling and hunting constitute the leonine part of the activity period. Even house cats that are allowed outdoors remain true to this heritage as they regularly patrol their territory. Indoor cats need to have enough to do indoors to remain well adjusted. Cats that can't regularly exercise their hunting instinct lose their mental equilibrium. They become maladjusted and act either apathetic or aggressive. If the uncomfortable situation

A new life with a new cat: the mistress of the domain is now more at ease with the little cat.

continues for quite a while, behavior abnormalities and illness may result. Fortunately, this is easy to avoid: Give your cat things to do, and provide a place where it can play games and sports. It will thank you with affection, a well-balanced nature, and joy in living.

In playing, cats develop all the techniques and movements they use in hunting. It doesn't matter if the mouse is real or not; in either case, the cat is just as engaged.

The Best Activity Programs

Single people's cats adapt their activity schedule to the daily routine of their owner: During work hours, the cat takes a substantial nap; when the owner returns, the cat is ready to go.

But cats rarely sleep for many hours without interruption. When they're awake they want exercise and something to do. That's a preventive measure for bad habits like uncleanliness, gnawing the carpet, and sharpening the claws on the sofa.

Running and climbing: From time to time the cat will enjoy a wild, galloping romp through the house. So before you leave the house, open all the doors to the rooms to make as long a racetrack as possible for the cat. Cats also like to go climbing. Be sure that the cat won't come to harm as it turns around on the bookcase or other pieces of furniture (e.g., because of a loose shelf), or cause any damage to vases, dishes, and pictures. Elevated, padded observation points make it especially stimulating to climb. Young cats like to exercise their climbing skills on curtains, so it would be a good idea to tie them up out of the way at first. Of course a scratching post is part of the basic equipment that belongs in every cat's home. It's useful for sharpening the claws, it's a piece of apparatus for climbing and gymnastics, and it's a lookout and a resting place.

Hide-and-seek: Curiosity and inquisitiveness turn cats into professional "hole experts." Bags, boxes, crates, and dark corners will all be thoroughly inspected. An empty moving box can be a favorite place for the cat; the rim of the box is good to gnaw on, and the cat will work at it with zeal and persistence. The play tunnels made of sisal that you can get in pet shops are also great fun for cats.

Boxes, tunnels, and blankets are ideal hiding places: The cat really likes it when it can look in them for treats or toys (see Practical Advice: Fun and Games, pages 50–51).

Hunting games: Everything that's small, light, and moveable triggers the desire to play: feathers, stuffed mice, Ping-Pong and rubber balls, balls of crumpled-up newspaper or aluminum foil, and pieces of wood or fabric. Cats especially enjoy trying to catch an object dragged along by a string, and they are fond of action games like using their paw to pull balls out of a box through little holes. Many cats can retrieve nearly as well as a dog, and they continually carry their favorite toy around with them.

Volleyball perfected: Cats are masterful ballplayers.

Cats are happy to play throughout their entire life. For cats that are alone in the house, play is the best remedy for frustration and boredom. But the greatest joy for a cat is a game that includes the human. Playing together strengthens the relationship between human and animal and is an expression of affection and attention. Here are the rules of play you should observe:

✔ You can offer to play, but it's the cat who accepts or declines.

✔ Cats say when they no longer feel like playing. Watch for these signals: a wagging tail, twitching fur on the back, ears laid back, and defensive use of paws or claws.

✔ Stop the game if playful attacks to the person's hands or feet become serious. Don't resume contact until the cat has calmed down.

✔ Avoid getting too close to cats that use their claws.

✔ Respect individual character traits. For example, many cats don't want to be touched on the belly, and they make that known by using their claws.

✔ Kittens and old cats need plenty of rest. Play in short intervals.

✔ Never disturb a sleeping cat and try to get it to play.

✔ The best times for play are late afternoon and evening, but not sooner than an hour after eating.

Ball Games and Toys on String

"Soccer:" Many cats will tirelessly kick small balls of all descriptions into the farthest corners of the room. Your job involves getting the ball back into play when the cat can't reach it.

Toys on a String: Swing a toy back and forth in front of the cat. As an alternative, you can use a spool or a cork on a string, or attach a rubber band to a stick.

Running, Jumping, and Balancing

Chase: Attach a spool, feather, or cork to a piece of yarn about a yard/meter long and pull it across the floor in a zigzag pattern. From time to time you should let the cat catch the prey.

A kitty box: Boxes and crates with windows cut into them are heaven on earth for little kittens.

High Jump: Hold a treat or a toy up high and have the cat jump up to get it. If you hold the object in your hand, you risk injury from the claws. It's a better idea to tie the object to a string.

A fun game for two: toys on a string develop reactions and dexterity.

Target Jump: Put treats on a chair or the sofa and encourage the cat to jump by saying, "Hop!" At the same time, pat the table or the sofa with your hand. If you practice daily, the cat will soon jump on command even with no further reward. Target jump with an obstacle: Put the treats on the floor behind an obstacle that's about eight inches/twenty cm high. You can gradually raise the height of the obstacle.

Balancing: Attach a strip of wood about an inch wide and a yard long (two to three cm by 100 cm) so that it spans two chairs. The strip must not move, tip, or wiggle. Once the cat jumps onto the chair, use a treat to encourage it to do a balancing act.

Sitting Up: Hold a treat about eight inches/ twenty cm over the cat's head to motivate it to sit up.

Hide-and-Seek

Searching for an object: In the cat's presence, hide a ball, squeak toy, or bundle of catnip (from the pet shop) under a blanket, towel, or rug. Reinforce the search behavior by saying "Seek!" Alternatively, the toy can be attached to a cord and moved under a blanket or through a tube. You can also hide a toy or a treat in a box and shake it to encourage the cat to look for it. If you cut some holes into a closed box, the cat will try to fish the object out with its paws.

Hiding: When the cat is not looking, hide in the closet or behind a door. Attract the cat by squeaking a toy, rustling some paper, or calling to it. Sometimes the roles can be reversed when the cat finds you. Then it will run and hide and wait for you to find it.

Fetch: Many cats will fetch anything that they can carry – from slippers to a rubber ball. And they'll wait until the owner throws it again. But be careful to avoid using objects that could get swallowed.

Little Tricks

Whether or not tricks are possible depends on your time, patience, reward system (treats and petting), and on always using the same commands.

Take a side roll, for example: Use a treat to get the cat to roll to one side when it's already lying on its back. Practice the move every day. Petting and rewarding the cat is very important in all games – even if the cat doesn't get it right.

CATS AND SENIOR CITIZENS: PARTNERS FOR LIFE

A cat is always there when we need it: It can be gentle, courteous, and loving. It is independent, and it places no great physical demands on people. Older people, especially ones who live alone, often see cats as much more than mere house pets.

Cats Bring Cheer

Cats have an exceptional physical presence. They move confidently, and they communicate elegance, warmth, and liveliness. The closeness of a cat has an immediate effect on a person's well-being: It banishes gloomy thoughts, melancholy, and depression; it motivates people to activity and laughter. A cat's demands are immediate and direct, and a person can't evade them. This direct type of confrontation sometimes draws lonely people out of the shell into which they have retreated. In many places cats have long been used as "associate therapists" and "social workers" in nursing homes, hospitals, and establishments for the disabled. People everywhere are learning to appreciate that cats cheer us up. Many of the millions and millions of cats in our households are partners with senior citizens.

A Common Sphere of Living: Cats are devoted to place. The close bonding with a relatively restricted living space predestines

them to being the ideal companion for older people. Generally, senior citizens are less mobile than younger people, and they place particular value on a comfortable and very personal home environment.

A Gentle and Sedate Routine: Older people rarely use frantic gestures and energetic movements; they tend to create little noise or chaos. In the eyes of a cat, those are distinctive pluses for a harmonious partnership.

A Stable Relationship: Among young people, living conditions and relationships can change quite quickly as a result of marriage, children, divorce, and changes in residence or work. That rarely occurs with senior citizens. The stability and continuity of such a partnership are guarantees for a happy relationship for the cat.

Respect and Tenderness: For older people, especially ones who live alone, a cat can take on a special meaning as a partner. It's often the focal point of a person's life. Senior citizens have a special respect for the demands and needs of a cat. Tender and courteous togetherness becomes the hallmark of the daily routine.

Tender devotion: In all ways, senior citizens are ideal parters for cats.

Considerations for Senior Citizens

House pets protect older people from loneliness and isolation, give their life a purpose, contribute affection and tenderness, structure the daily routine, provide conversational material, and keep memories alive. But house pets also involve duties and responsibilities, and cost money and time. Therefore, senior citizens should consider the following questions before they get a cat:

✔ Are you sufficiently fit to provide the daily care that a cat needs? That includes regular shopping for food and taking the animal to the vet. Who will bring the cat to

the vet if you don't have your own car? Does your vet make house calls?

✔ Are there people in your circle of acquaintances who could take adequate care of your cat in case of emergency?

✔ Cats cost money: care, food, and medications, accessories, veterinary costs, a cat sitter, and a "nest egg" could amount to several hundred dollars in a year's time. Can you handle these expenses without cutting back in other areas?

✔ Who will care for the cat if you become ill for a long time or can't take care of it any longer? What arrangements are in place in case you pass away?

✔ In case a move to a nursing home is part of the plan, will you be able to take your cat with you?

✔ The requirements of cats and people don't always coincide; will you be able to put up with it if the cat sometimes wakes up in the middle of the night, or becomes stubborn or excessively vocal when it's in heat? (If you don't intend to breed your cat, you surely should have it neutered; see page 23.)

✔ Purebred cats that require a lot of care, or that are very lively, such as Persians and Siamese, respectively, require lots of involvement, patience, and time. Can you handle these special demands for ten, fifteen, or more years?

✔ Kittens need almost around-the-clock care and attention during the first few weeks – including in the middle of the night. Are you willing and able to deal with this?

Loving companions: Seniors and cats do almost everything together.

Purebred Cats for Senior Citizens

Many older people have pulled back from the hustle and bustle and the noise of daily life. It's understandable that they would search for a calm and well-adjusted partner in their house pet. The following chart of breeds focuses on cats with a particularly gentle and playful nature. People who are looking for something a little livelier may find their dream cat in the breeds that are designated with an asterisk.

Name	Type	Temperament	Characteristics
Abyssinian*	slender but robust shorthaired cat	receptive and friendly with people, active, and playful	easy to care for, needs plenty to keep it busy and entertain it
British Shorthair	compact breed; cross between Persian and English house cat	well adjusted, affectionate, and friendly	very devoted, subdued temperament
Burmese*	slender type with muscular build	pleasant, playful, alert, and gentle	smooth coat easily groomed; great variety of colors
Exotic Shorthair	stocky type with powerful legs, round head	people oriented, good-natured, gentle, and playful	more calm than other breeds, even as a kitten; easy to care for
Holy Birman	powerful; long, silky fur, white "gloves"	alert, gentle, and quiet	Birmans like tender cuddling
Persian	Longhaired cat with thick fur	very calm, sedate, needs little exercise	indoor cat, daily coat care very important
Rag Doll	imposing and stable medium-longhaired cat	very quiet, composed, and sociable	calm, composed nature makes it an ideal cat for senior citizens
Siamese*	very slender, graceful, long-legged shorthaired type	very devoted and active, but often very vocal	Siamese give their owners their all, but can get on people's nerves; for experienced cat owners
Turkish Angora	slender, attractive medium-longhaired cat	lively, playful, and curious	despite its lively nature, sociable and lovable

Abyssinians, Burmese, and Siamese form a close bond with their humans, but at the same time are very active and demanding. To prevent boredom, they are best kept in pairs.

Note: The individual differences in temperament (devotion, curiosity, and playfulness, for example) can be greater than the differences between breeds.

Who Will Help Care for My Cat in an Emergency?

For many cats, living with an older person is heaven on earth; the owner pampers and spoils them, because caring for a cat gives the person's daily routine meaning and purpose. Also, after the human has lost a partner, a pet is often the only living being that's close to them. If this close relationship becomes impossible because of the owner's illness or disability in the short or long term, it can turn into a dramatic situation for both person and cat.

So senior citizens in particular shouldn't put off looking around for a responsible person with cat experience who could take over if needed.

By our side even through the night: many senior citizens allow their cat to sleep with them.

Relatives, Friends, and Neighbors: The surrogate care will work out best if the cat already knows its caretaker, and if that person knows the cat's preferences and characteristics. That's often the case with relatives, friends, and neighbors. The cat should be cared for in its familiar surroundings, for senior citizens' cats in particular form a strong tie to their home. Go over all the details with the caregiver and post a note containing the most important information: the usual food, any medications, special considerations, favorite games, and address and phone number of your veterinarian. Show the caregiver where to find this information and the cat's shot record.

Veterinarian: If there is no caregiver in your immediate area, your vet can make the necessary arrangements. Discuss your situation and the cat's needs with the veterinarian. That person will almost always be in contact with cat lovers who can care for an animal at least temporarily. Keep your vet's phone number handy and leave a note to call the vet in case of emergency.

Cat Associations: Many cities and counties have cat clubs. You'll always find a receptive audience when you look around for someone to take care of your cat. Contact club members in advance to get addresses of cat lovers with whom your cat would feel comfortable.

Breeders: Breeders of purebred cats are usually prepared to care for cats.

My Cat Does Whatever It Wants!

Senior citizens are not exempt from having problem cats. A common cause for that is older people's willingness to let the cat have its way.

✔ Love for a house pet is often expressed at the food dish. A disproportionately high percentage of overweight cats live in the households of senior citizens. Even though obesity is less of a problem with cats than with dogs, which are runners and may

develop skeletal problems, animals that are fat suffer more frequently from diabetes and bladder stones. Special diet food is recommended for overweight animals; it's available from veterinarians and pet shops.

✔ Cats that always get their way can act rebellious and aggressive if you suddenly try to impose some new limit. For example, a cat that is used to sleeping on the bed won't be very understanding if it has to keep away because of the owner's illness.

✔ The battle over food: Spoiled cats have their own ideas about food. If the favorite food isn't available, a cat will refuse to eat – sometimes for days. Older owners may not know what to do in such situations and may bend to the will of the cat. Of course, you can offer your cat some variety in the food dish, but the choice should still be up to the person. Give your cat the food it's used to. If it doesn't eat it, take the dish away after thirty minutes. Repeat this process at the accustomed mealtimes.

An undisturbed siesta in bed is a source of happiness for cats.

How to Achieve Togetherness

Older people and cats have one thing in common: They structure their day according to individual preferences and habits. With senior citizens that can be the morning walk, a siesta after lunch, or afternoon tea; with cats, the nine o'clock patrol through the territory, an eleven o'clock catnap for digesting, and a thorough cat bath in the evening. There is nothing better for both of them than doing certain customary things together and discovering new preferences in common.

For example, every feeding can turn into a little celebration. Serve your cat its dinner precisely on the minute. Stay close by, but without disturbing the cat. Usually it will interrupt its meal to rub its head or sides against you as a way of thanks. After the meal, take some time to cuddle with the cat or to enjoy a snooze together. You can even treat your cat to a meal that you prepare yourself. But don't forget that in culinary matters, cats are dyed-in-the-wool creatures of habit.

There are many daily activities that cats can do with their owners.

✔ Reading a book or a newspaper together: The cat can sit on your lap or the chair arm.

✔ Taking a walk together: The cat can trot along (on the way to the mailbox, for example), or go for a walk on a leash; a harness is the best choice for this.

At Ease in Meeting Family

Your children and grandchildren come to visit on the weekend. That's no treat for the cat, which knows only its tranquil life with you. Shy cats prefer to slip away and reappear only after the visitors leave. Others protest through scratching, biting, or uncleanliness. So try to avoid

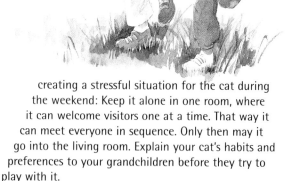

creating a stressful situation for the cat during the weekend: Keep it alone in one room, where it can welcome visitors one at a time. That way it can meet everyone in sequence. Only then may it go into the living room. Explain your cat's habits and preferences to your grandchildren before they try to play with it.

Promptly at the door: Cats operate according to a fixed schedule.

Many cats are happy to walk on a lead.

✔ Writing letters together: The cat can lie on the desk.
✔ Working together in the garden: The cat helps out as you turn over the soil in the springtime.
✔ Taking a bath together: The cat will test the water temperature from the edge of the bathtub.

Petting Games and Cuddling
Wild games usually aren't the choice of older people. The alternative is just fine with the cat: games that involve petting and cuddling.
✔ Hide behind an open door and call the cat. When the cat finds you, the petting and little treats are more important than the action.

A magic cure for stress: a favorite book, a favorite chair, and a cat on the lap.

✔ Many cats like to lie on a person's neck and shoulders and go for a walk. The two of you can go on journeys of discovery through the house and yard.
✔ The balcony seat by the window is fascinating to all cats. Gazing out the window together is twice the fun. Sit with your cat at the window and enjoy the view. That's another good opportunity to cuddle.
✔ This is a daily duty with longhaired cats, but it's good fun with other cats as well: Groom your cat with a brush and comb, and that will automatically provide some petting.
✔ A brief midday nap refreshes you both for the rest of the day. Save a place next to you on the couch so the cat can join you.

Page numbers in bold print refer to color
photos or illustrations.

62 A P P E N D I X

Helpful Addresses
• American Association of Cat Enthusiasts (AACE)
P.O. Box 213
Pine Brook, NJ 07058
(201) 335-6717
• American Cat Association (ACA)
8101 Catherine Avenue
Panorama City, CA 91402
(818) 781-5656
• American Cat Fanciers Association (ACFA)
P.O. Box 304
Pt. Lookout, MO 65726
(417) 334-5430
• Canadian Cat Association (CCA)
83 Kennedy Road, Unit 1806
Brampton, Ontario
Canada L6W 3P3

Other Organizations and Animal Protection Agencies
• American Society for the Prevention of Cruelty to Animals (ASPCA)
424 East 92nd Street
New York, NY 10128
(212) 876 -7700
• Friends of Animals
P.O. Box 1244
Norwalk, CT 06856
(800) 631-2212
(for low-cost spay/ neuter program information)

• The Humane Society of the United States (HSUS)
2100 L Street NW
Washington, DC 20037
(202) 452-1100
• Pets Are Wonderful Support (PAWS)
P.O. Box 460489
San Francisco, CA 94146
(415) 241-1460
(provides pet-related services for people with AIDS)

Cat Magazines
• *Cats*
P.O. Box 420240
Palm Coast, FL 32142-0240
(904) 445-2818
• *Cat Fancy*
P.O. Box 52864
Boulder, CO 52864
(714) 855-8822
• *Cat Fancier's Almanac*
1805 Atlantic Avenue
P.O. Box 1105
Manasquan, NJ 08736-0805
(908) 528-9797
Catnip (newsletter)
Tufts University School of Veterinary Medicine
P.O. Box 420014
Palm Coast, FL 32142-0014
(800) 829-0926

Books for Further Reading
• Behrend, K. *Indoor Cats.* Hauppauge, NY: Barron's Educational Series, Inc., 1999.
• Behrend, K. and Wegler, Monika. *The Complete Book of Cat Care.* Hauppauge, New York: Barron's Educational Series, Inc., 1991.
• Daly, Carol Himsel, D.V.M. *Caring for Your Sick Cat.* Hauppauge, New York: Barron's Educational Series, Inc., 1994.
• Frye, Fredric. *First Aid for Your Cat.* Hauppauge, New York: Barron's Educational Series, Inc., 1987.
• Head, Honor. *101 Questions Your Cat Would Ask.* Hauppauge, New York: Barron's Educational Series, Inc., 1999.

• Maggitti, Phil. *Guide to a Well Behaved Cat.* Hauppauge, New York: Barron's Educational Series, Inc., 1993.
• Viner, Bradley, D.V.M. *The Cat Care Manual.* Hauppauge, New York: Barron's Educational Series, Inc., 1993.
• Wright, M. and S. Walters, eds. *The Book of the Cat.* New York: Summit Books, 1980.

Author

Zoologist and journalist Dr. Gerd Ludwig is an author of books about house pets and a freelance reporter.

Illustrator

György Jankovics is a trained illustrator who studied at the Budapest and Hamburg art academies.

Photographer

All photos are by Ulrike Schanz, except for the following: front cover (small photo): Gisela Caspersen, Juniors Photo Archive. Ulrike Schanz works as a freelance photo designer and has specialized in animal portraits for several years.

Translator

Eric A. Bye, M.A., is a cat owner and freelance translator who works in rural Vermont.

Photos: Book Cover and Inside

Front cover: Young Persian Cat (left) and Norwegian Forest Cat (right) (large photo).
Young woman with house cat (small photo).
Back cover: Tiger and marmalade house cats.
Page 1: Girl cuddling with a Norwegian Forest Cat.
Pages 2-3: Gray and reddish tiger house cats.
Pages 4-5: Cats are interested in mice in all forms.
Pages 6-7: Kittens from the same litter.
Pages 64-65: Black and white house cat.

Thanks

The author and publisher thank Mrs. Elina Sistonen for proofreading the text.

Copyright

English translation Copyright © 2001 by Barron's Educational Series, Inc.
Published originally under the title MEINE TRAUMKATZE
Copyright © 2000 by Gräfe und Unzer Verlag GmbH, München
English Translation by Eric A. Bye

All inquiries should be addressed to:
Barron's Educational Series, Inc.
250 Wireless Boulevard
Hauppauge, New York 11788
http://www.barronseduc.com
Library of Congress Catalog Card No. 00-110921
International Standard Book No. 0-7641-1876-5

Printed in Hong Kong
9 8 7 6 5 4 3 2 1

1 How can I find my dream cat?

Before you get a cat, talk to cat owners and breeders and cat association members; read books and cat magazines, and search for information on the Internet.

2 What are the advantages of a young cat – or an older cat?

Kittens require lots of time, patience, and attention. You have to build up a very strong sense of trust. Grown cats have a mind of their own and particular habits.

3 I'm a single person and will have to leave the cat alone for several hours every day. Is that all right?

A cat should not be left alone for longer than four to six hours at the very most. Provide some toys and things for the cat to do so it will have some variety, or get a second cat to keep it company.

4 Should I have my cat neutered?

Every cat that is not going to be bred should be neutered. That's the only thing that will eliminate the misery of the many roaming cats.

5 How do I know whether I'll like having a cat?

Before you get a cat, find out what cats need; talk with experts and observe cats that your friends and acquaintances own.

An expert answers the ten most commonly asked questions about your dream cat.